WHAT'S IT REALLY LIKE TO BE AN ELECTRICIAN?

CHRISTINE HONDERS

PowerKiDS press.

New York

Published in 2020 by The Rosen Publishing Group, Inc.
29 East 21st Street, New York, NY 10010

First Edition

Editor: Greg Roza
Book Design: Michael Flynn

Photo Credits: Cover, p. 1 Monty Rakusen/Cultura/Getty Images; pp. 4, 6, 8, 10, 12, 14, 16, 18, 20, 22 (background) Apostrophe/Shutterstock.com; p. 5 Samson Yury/Shutterstock.com; p. 7 PT Hamilton/Shutterstock.com; p. 9 Jim Parkin/Shutterstock.com; p. 11 Huntstock/Getty Images; p. 13 KikoStock/Shutterstock.com; p. 15 anurakss/Shutterstock.com; p. 17 PRESSLAB/Shutterstock.com; p. 19 Roger Ressmeyer/Corbis/VCG/Corbis Documentary/Getty Images; p. 21 Zivica Kerkez/Shutterstock.com; p. 22 Volodymyr Krasyuk/Shutterstock.com.

Cataloging-in-Publication Data

Names: Honders, Christine.
Title: What's it really like to be an electrician? / Christine Honders.
Description: New York : PowerKids Press, 2020. | Series: Jobs kids want | Includes glossary and index.
Identifiers: ISBN 9781538349847 (pbk.) | ISBN 9781538349861 (library bound) | ISBN 9781538349854 (6 pack)
Subjects: LCSH: Electricians–Juvenile literature. | Electrical engineering–Vocational guidance–Juvenile literature. | Electric industries–Vocational guidance–Juvenile literature.
Classification: LCC TK159.H66 2020 | DDC 621.3023–dc23

Manufactured in the United States of America

CPSIA Compliance Information: Batch #CSPK19. For Further Information contact Rosen Publishing, New York, New York at 1-800-237-9932.

CONTENTS

The Power of Electricity

You turn on the lights. You grab a snack from the refrigerator. You play your favorite video game. Do you ever think about how these things all work? They all work because of electricity. They work because electricians keep working!

Where Does Electricity Come From?

Electricity is a form of **energy**. Power plants make electricity by burning coal, oil, or natural gas. This makes heat, which is used to boil water. Steam from the boiling water powers machines called generators. Running water is also used to power generators. Generators make electricity.

generators

Power Lines

Electricity moves through wires called power lines. Power lines bring electricity to our businesses and homes. Electricians make sure electricity goes where it's supposed to, and that it keeps going. Sometimes they need to fix power lines after a storm.

Electricians at Work

Electricians make sure the power works in our homes and in public places. They fix wires in old buildings and set up electricity in new buildings. Electricians can also work outside. They make sure the power lines to and from power plants are working.

Team Players

Electricians are sometimes part of a team. Builders get help from electricians when they're making a new home. They work together to plan and to **install** the wires. New electricians are trained by experienced electricians. They work in teams to learn from each other.

On the Move

Being an electrician means being on the move! They're often on their feet, going from job to job. Electricians climb **utility poles** and fix wires up in the air. They often need to climb ladders and **scaffolds**. They shouldn't be afraid of heights.

Brain Power!

Electricians are good problem solvers. They test and study electrical **systems** to figure out which part isn't working. They know basic math and how to read building plans. Electricians must have steady hands when working on tiny parts.

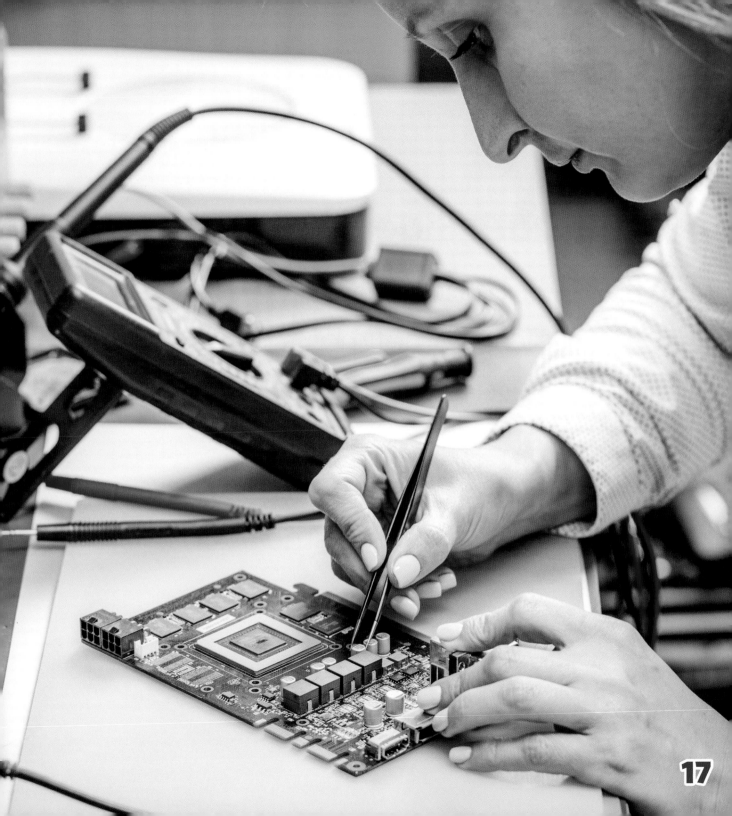

The Dark Side

Electricians have to watch out for their safety. Sometimes they work in tight spaces or in high places. They work with dangerous live wires. Some electricians also need to be ready to work at any time in case an emergency happens.

How Can I Become an Electrician?

You can become an electrician right after high school if you take **algebra**. You'll learn while you work with an experienced electrician for up to five years. In most places, electricians have to pass a test before they can work on their own. Then, you'll be an electrician!

Lighting It Up!

Electricians are like detectives. They figure out what's wrong and how to fix it. It's an exciting job where there's always something new to learn. The world runs on electricity and we need electricians to keep lighting everything up!

GLOSSARY

algebra: A kind of math that uses letters to stand for missing numbers in an equation.

energy: The power to work or act.

install: To set up or put in place.

scaffold: A raised surface built as a support for workers and their tools.

system: The way a group of people or things work together.

utility pole: A tall pole used to support telephone and power lines.

INDEX

WEBSITES

Due to the changing nature of Internet links, PowerKids Press has developed an online list of websites related to the subject of this book. This site is updated regularly. Please use this link to access the list: www.powerkidslinks.com/JKW/electrician